Abbreviations

approx approximately

beg begin(ning)

BO bind off

CC contrasting color

cm centimeters

CO cast on

cont continue

dec decrease

dpn double-pointed needle(s)

g grams

inc increase

k knit

k1f&b knit into front and back loop of same stitch

k2tog knit two stitches together

kwise knitwise

MC main color

M1 increase 1 by inserting the left hand needle under the horizontal thread between the stitch just worked and the next st; knit into the back of the resulting loop to make a stitch

mm millimeters

p purl

p1f&b purl into front and back loop of same stitch

p2tog purl two stitches together

patt pattern

pm place marker

psso pass slipped st over

pwise purlwise

rem remain(ing)

rep repeat

rib ribbing

rnd(s) rounds

RS right side

SK2P slip 1, k2tog, pass slipped st over (a left leaning double decrease)

sl slip

ssk slip the first and second stitches one at a time kwise, then insert left hand needle into the fronts of these stitches and knit them together

ssp slip first and second stitches one at a time kwise, then slip them back to the left hand needle; insert the right hand needle through the back loops of the two stitches (going into the second stitch first), then purl them together

st(s) stitch(es)

St st Stockinette stitch (k on RS, p on WS)

tbl through back loop

WS wrong side

wyib with yarn in back

wyif with yarn in front

yo yarn over needle

* repeat from *

[] repeat instructions in brackets as directed

Roly-Poly Ridges

Design by Bonnie Franz

This simple-to-knit hat is the perfect first project to work in the round. The gentle roll of the brim is stopped with ribbing, which helps keep the hat on the baby's head! Garter ridges add both color and texture.

Roly-Poly Ridges

Size: 12 to 18 months
Head circumference: 16" (40.5 cm)

YARN

 Lightweight smooth yarn
(A): approx 90 yd (82.3 m),
(B): approx 15 yd (13.7 m),
(C): approx 40 yd (36.6 m),
(D): approx 8 yd (7.3 m)

Shown: Lion Brand *Baby Soft;* 60%
acrylic, 40% nylon; 5 oz (140 g)/459 yd
(420 m): 1 ball each #920-170 Pistachio
Green (A), #920-156 Pastel Green (B),
#920-100 White (C), #920-157 Pastel
Yellow (D)

NEEDLES AND NOTIONS

One size 6 (4.0 mm) circular needle
16" (40 cm) long, or size needed to
get gauge

One set size 6 (4.0 mm) dpns, or size
needed to get gauge

One pair size 6 (4.0 mm) knitting
needles, or size needed to get gauge

Ten stitch markers, one in a different
color to mark beg of rnd

One blunt-end yarn needle

GAUGE

20 sts and 28 rows = 4" (10 cm) over
St st worked in the round

Stripe sequence

(work twice)

K 5 rnds A, k 1 rnd B, p 1 rnd B, k 5 rnds C, k 1 rnd D, p 1 rnd D.

HAT

*This hat is worked in the round. Switch to double-pointed
needles when the stitches no longer fit comfortably on the
circular needle.*

Brim

With the circular needle and A, CO 80 sts. Join, being careful not
to twist sts. Place a marker (pm) on the needle to indicate beg of
rnd, and slip the marker every rnd. Knit 5 rnds, then work 2 rnds
in k1, p1 rib. Begin the stripe sequence and inc one st on first
rnd—81 sts. Work even in stripe sequence until piece measures
$3\frac{1}{2}$" (8.9 cm) from ribbing.

Crown

Continue with stripe sequence until it has been worked twice, then
work in St st with A only.

Next (dec setup) rnd *K7, k2tog, pm; rep from * around—72 sts.

Next 2 rnds Work even in patt as established.

Next (dec) rnd *Knit to 2 sts before marker, k2tog, slip marker; rep
from * around.

Rep last 3 rnds 5 times—18 sts.

Next rnd Knit.

Next rnd [K2tog] around, removing dec markers—9 sts.

Next rnd [K2tog] around, ending k1—5 sts.

Cut yarn, leaving a 6" (15.2 cm) tail.

Use a yarn needle to pull the tail through the rem sts twice, pull
tight, and secure tail on WS.

Weave in all ends.

BOOTIES

Make two. These booties are knitted flat from sole up, then sewn together.

Sole

With A, CO 16 sts, pm, CO 1 st, pm, CO 16 sts. Knit 1 row—33 sts.

Inc Row K1, M1, knit to marker, M1, slip marker, k1, M1, knit to last st, M1, k1—37 sts.

Rep Inc Row twice more—45 sts. Remove markers.

Knit 3 rows.

Instep

Next 5 rows Beg with a RS row and cont with A, work in St st.

Next row (WS) P21, pm, p3, pm, p21.

Dec Row 1 Knit to 2 sts before marker, ssk, slip marker, k3, k2tog, knit to end—43 sts.

Dec Row 2 Purl to 2 sts before marker, p2tog, slip marker, p3, ssp, purl to end—41 sts.

Rep Dec Rows 1 and 2 three more times—29 sts rem. Remove markers.

Next 2 rows With B, knit. Break off B.

Next 5 rows With C, beg with a RS row, work in St st.

Next 2 rows With D, purl. Break off D.

Next 3 rows With A, purl 1 row, then work 2 rows in k1, p1 rib.

Next 6 rows With A, work in St st.

BO all sts loosely. Break off A, leaving an 8" (20.3 cm) tail for seaming.

Finishing

Fold the bootie in half and sew the sole and back seams.

Weave in all ends.

To make the tie, CO 100 sts with C, then BO all sts.

Using a yarn needle, weave the tie through the ridge at ankle on bootie (see photo); tie in a bow.

Stockinette stitch rolls toward the knit side to form the brim.

Ties are woven through the stitches at the ankle.

Grape Fizz

Design by Bonnie Franz

"Mistake stitch" ribbing gives great texture, but is simple and quick to knit. The drawstring design of the hat makes finishing easy. White edging adds the fizz.

Mistake rib stitch pattern

(multiple of 4 sts + 3)

Row 1 *K2, p2; rep from * to last 3 sts, ending k2, p1.

Rep row 1.

HAT

This hat is worked flat and seamed.

Brim to crown

With CC, CO 91 sts. Work 1 row in Mistake Rib. Change to MC and work even in patt as established for 7" (17.8 cm).

Cut yarn, leaving a 6" (5.2 cm) tail. Use a yarn needle to thread tail through sts twice; pull tight and secure to WS.

Finishing

Seam the back of the hat.

Weave in all ends.

BOOTIES

Make two. These booties are begun flat, then worked in the round.

Cuff

With CC, CO 31 sts. Work 1 row in Mistake Rib. Change to MC and work even in patt as established until piece measures 2" (5.1 cm) from beg, ending with a WS row, and inc 1 st on last row—32 sts.

Heel flap

Slip sts to dpns as follows: place 8 sts on the first dpn; place next 16 sts on the second dpn (instep sts); place last 8 sts on the first dpn.

Next 11 rows Slipping the first st of each row pwise, work back and forth in St st on the 16 sts on the first needle only.

Turn heel

Row 1 (WS) Sl 1, p8, p2tog, p1, turn.

Row 2 Sl 1, k3, ssk, k1, turn.

Row 3 Sl 1, p4, p2tog, p1, turn.

Row 4 Sl 1, k5, ssk, k1, turn.

Row 5 Sl 1, p6, p2tog, p1, turn.

Row 6 Sl 1, k7, ssk, k1.

Gusset

Pick up and knit 6 sts along side of heel flap. With the free dpn, knit across 16 sts on second needle. With a third dpn, pick up and knit 6 sts along other side of heel flap, then cont across first needle—22 sts on first needle, 16 sts on second needle.

Rnd 1 Knit all sts.

Rnd 2 On the first needle, k1, ssk, knit across to last 3 sts, k2tog, k1; on the second needle, knit all sts.

Rep these 2 rnds until 32 sts rem—16 sts on each needle.

Next 7 rnds Knit.

Toe

Rnd 1 Knit all sts.

Rnd 2 On the first needle,* k1, ssk, knit to last 3 sts, k2tog, k1; rep from * on the second needle. Rep these 2 rnds until 12 sts rem—6 sts on each needle.

Graft sts together.

Tie

Using a crochet hook and CC, crochet a chain 15" (38.1 cm) long, leaving 4" (10.1 cm) tails at beg and end. Thread through ribs just above heel flap. Tie in a bow. *Note: If you don't want to crochet a chain, you could use ribbon or make a braid.*

Mistake rib is very stretchy.

Sock-style booties have mistake-rib cuffs.

Soft and Simple

Design by Edie Eckman

Who can resist a happy baby wearing a soft, plush hat-and-bootie set? This hat is super easy to make—it's just garter stitch! The booties are a sock mini-workshop; you can learn the basics of socks in an hour or less and have something for the baby when you are done.

HAT

Slip all stitches purlwise.

Brim to crown

Loosely CO 42 sts.

Work in garter stitch until the hat measures 7" (17.8 cm) from beg. BO.

Finishing

Sew the side and top seams.

Pull the top corners to the center of the top seam and tack them together.

Weave in all ends.

BOOTIES

Make two.

Cuff

With dpns, loosely CO 16 sts. Place a marker on needle to indicate beg of rnd, and slip marker every rnd.

Rnds 1, 3 and 5 Knit.

Rnds 2, 4 and 6 Purl.

Heel flap

Worked on 8 sts only.

Rows 1–9 K8, turn.

Turn heel

Row 1 K4, ssk, k1; turn, leaving one st unworked.

Row 2 Sl 1, k1, ssk, k1; turn, leaving one st unworked.

Row 3 Sl 1, k2, ssk; turn.

Row 4 K3, ssk—4 sts.

Gusset

Pickup rnd On one needle, pick up and knit 5 sts along the heel flap; on a second needle, k8 instep sts; on a third needle, pick up and knit 5 sts along the other side of the heel flap, k2 from the heel flap; place a marker to indicate beg of rnd—22 sts total sts, arranged on 3 needles 7-8-7.

Rnd 1 Purl.

Rnd 2 On the first needle, knit to last 2 sts, k2tog; on the second needle, knit across the instep sts; on the third needle, ssk, knit to the end of the rnd—20 sts.

Rnd 3 Purl.

Rnds 4-5 Rep Rnds 2-3—18 sts.

Rnds 6-7 Rep Rnds 2-3—16 sts.

Cont working garter stitch in-the-round (knit 1 rnd, purl 1 rnd) until the foot measures approx 4½" (11.4 cm) from the back of the heel.

Toe

[K2, k2tog] around—12 sts. Purl 1 rnd.

[K2tog] around—6 sts. Cut yarn.

With a yarn needle, thread the tail through the rem sts and pull tight.

Finishing

Weave in all ends.

If desired, thread elastic through the garter ridge on the inside of the bootie cuff and tie the ends together.

With this textured yarn, the garter-stitch pattern can't be seen.

Top corners of the rectangular hat are tacked together to give it a cute shape.

Elf

Design by Edie Eckman

This cute combo uses slip stitches for easy two-color knitting. The short-row shaping on the instep is especially fun to knit.

Elf

Size: 12 months
Head circumference:
15" (38.1 cm)

YARN

3 LIGHT Lightweight smooth yarn
(MC): approx 140 yd (128 m), (CC):
approx 40 yd (36.6 m)

NEEDLES AND NOTIONS

One pair size 6 (4.0 mm) needles, or
size needed to get gauge

Set of size 6 (4.0 mm) dpns, or size
needed to get gauge

Blunt-end yarn needle

GAUGE

22 sts and 28 rows = 4"
(10 cm) in St st

Broken ridges stitch pattern

(multiple of 4 sts + 1)

Note: Slip all stitches purlwise.

Row 1 (RS) With MC, knit.

Row 2 Purl.

Row 3 With CC, k1, *k3, sl 1; rep from *, end last rep k1.

Row 4 P1, *k3, sl 1 wyif; rep from *, end last rep p1.

Row 5 With MC, k2, *sl 1, k3; rep from *, end last rep k2.

Rows 6 and 8 Purl.

Row 7 Knit.

Row 9 With CC, k2, *sl 1, k3; rep from *, end last rep k2.

Row 10 P1, k1, *sl 1 wyif, k3; rep from *, end last rep k1, p1.

Row 11 With MC, k1, *k3, sl 1; rep from *, end last rep k1.

Row 12 Purl.

Rep Rows 1–12.

Solid ridges stitch pattern

(any number)

Rows 1 and 2 With CC, knit.

Rows 3 and 5 (RS) With MC, knit.

Rows 4 and 6 With MC, purl.

Rep Rows 1–6.

HAT

This hat is worked flat, then seamed. Carry color not in use up the side of the fabric.

Brim to crown

With CC, loosely CO 81 sts.

Row 1 (WS) Knit.

Row 2 With MC, knit.

Row 3 *P2, k2; rep from *, ending with p1.

Rows 4 K1, *p2, k2; rep from *.

Rows 5–7 Cont in rib patt as established.

Work Broken Ridges patt for 20 rows, ending with Row 8.

Begin working Solid Ridges patt, and dec on Row 5, then every sixth row as follows (the decs will always occur on Row 5 of the pattern):

Dec row 1 K4, *k2 tog, k6; rep from *, ending the last rep k3—71 sts.

Dec row 2 K1, *ssk, k5; rep from * to the end of the row—61 sts.

Dec row 3 K2, *k2tog, k4; rep from *, ending the last rep k3—51 sts.

Dec row 4 K2, *ssk, k3; rep from *, ending the last rep k2—41 sts.

Dec row 5 K1, *k2tog, k2; rep from * to the end of the row—31 sts.

Dec row 6 K1, *ssk, k1; rep from * to end of row—21 sts.

Dec row 7 *K2tog; rep from *, ending with k1—11 sts.

Dec row 8 K1, [ssk] to the end of the row—6 sts.

Cut yarn, leaving a 24" (61 cm) tail for seaming. Thread yarn through the rem sts and pull tight.

Finishing

Sew the back seam.

Weave in all ends.

Slipped stitches of the broken ridges stitch pattern carry the off-white yarn up to the next row.

BOOTIES

Make two. This bootie is worked from the sole to the cuff. Parts of it are worked in the round.

Sole

With MC, CO 6 sts onto one dpn.

Row 1 K1f&b, k4, k1f&b—8 sts.

Working back and forth, knit every row until sole measures 4" (10.2 cm) from beg.

Next (Dec) row K2tog, k4, k2tog—6 sts.

Knit one row.

Foot

With a second needle, pick up and knit 22 sts along the long side of the sole; with a third needle, pick up and knit 6 sts; with a fourth needle, pick up and knit 22 sts along the other long side of the sole—56 sts.

Rnd 1 With CC, knit.

Rnd 2 Purl.

Rnds 3–5 With MC, knit.

Rnd 6 With CC, *sl 1, k3; rep from * to the end of the row.

Rnd 7 *Sl 1, k3; rep from *.

Rnd 8 With MC, *k2, sl 1, k1; rep from * to the end of the row.

Rnds 9–10 Knit.

Rnd 11 With CC, knit.

Row 12 Purl.

Rnd 13 With MC, knit.

Instep

Knit 7, turn, leaving the rem sts unworked.

*K2tog, k7, turn; rep from * until 28 sts rem. Do not turn at end of last row.

Knit 1 rnd.

Cuff

Work in k1, p1 rib for 2" (5.1 cm). BO loosely.

Finishing

Weave in all ends.

Garter-stitch sole is worked flat. Then stitches are picked up around the sole on dpns to begin working in the round.

Ribbons and Bows

Design by Debby Ware

Your baby will be dressed to the nines with this ribbon-topped hat on her head. This is a simple project—just work a tube in the round, add a drawstring on top, and pull!

Seed stitch pattern

(multiple of 2 sts)

Row 1 *K1, p1; rep from * to end of row.

Row 2 Purl each knit st and knit each purl st.

Rep Row 2.

HAT

This hat is worked in the round.

Brim

With circular needle and C, CO 90 sts. Join, being careful not to twist sts. Place a marker on the needle to indicate the beg of rnd, and slip marker every rnd.

Rnd 1 Purl.

Rnd 2 Attach A. *K1, sl 1 wyib; rep from * to end of rnd.

Rnd 3 With A, *p1, sl 1 wyib; rep from * to end of rnd.

Rnd 4 With C, knit.

Rnd 5 With C, purl.

Rnd 6 Attach B. Rep Rnd 2.

Rnds 7–9 With B, rep Rnds 3 thru 5.

Rnds 10–14 With A, then C, rep Rnds 2–5. Cut C.

Next 2 rnds With B, knit one rnd, then purl one rnd.

Next 5 rnds With A, knit.

Rep previous 7 rnds 4 more times. Cut B.

Next 2 rnds Attach D. Knit 1 rnd, then purl 1 rnd.

Next rnd With A, knit.

Next rnd (Eyelet rnd) With A, *k4, yo, k2tog; rep from * to end of rnd.

Next rnd With A, knit.

Next 2 rnds With D, knit 1 rnd, then purl 1 rnd. Cut D.

Attach E and, holding A and E together, work seed st for 2"

(5 cm). Cut E.

With A, BO all sts. Cut A.

Ribbons and Bows
Size: 6 months to 2 years
Head circumference: 14" (35.6 cm)

YARN

3 LIGHT Lightweight smooth yarn
A (purple): approx 160 yd (146.3 m),
B (green): approx 80 yd (73.4 m),
C (yellow): approx 90 yd (82.3 m),
D (pink): approx 10 yd (9.1 m)

4 MEDIUM Medium weight novelty yarn tufted with ribbons and eyelash (E): approx 60 yds (54.9 m)

NEEDLES AND NOTIONS

One pair size 3 (3.25 mm) knitting needles

One size 4 (3.5 mm) circular needle 16" (40 cm) long, or size needed to get gauge

Two small stitch holders

One blunt-end yarn needle

GAUGE

22 sts and 28 rows = 4" (10 cm) over St st using cotton yarn

Hat is knitted flat and then sewn into a tube. A drawstring gathers the top into a riot of ribbons.

Slipped stitches carry the yellow yarn into the periwinkle and green rows to give the brim band a checkered look.

Finishing

Weave in all ends.

Using a yarn needle, carefully poke and pull all those little ribbon ends that have ended up on the inside of the hat to the outside.

Make a 3-st I-cord tie (page 30), approx 22" (55.9 cm) long. Weave the tie through the eyelets. Make a knot at each end of the cord to keep it from slipping out of the eyelets. Tie in a big bow.

BOOTIES

Make two. These booties are worked flat from the cuff down, then seamed.

Cuff

With smaller needles and A, CO 36 sts.

First 3 rows Attach E and holding A and E together, work in seed stitch. Cut E.

Next 2 rows With A, knit 1 row, then purl 1 row.

Next row (Eyelet row) K2, *yo, k2tog, k4*; rep from * to last 4 sts, ending last rep yo, k2tog, k2.

Next row Purl.

Next 7 rows Work k2, p1 rib.

Instep

Next row (WS) K24, turn. Put the 12 unworked sts on a holder.

Next row Attach B. K12, turn. Put the 12 unworked sts on a second holder.

Next 12 rows Work in seed stitch on these 12 sts only. Cut B.

Foot

Next row With RS facing, attach C at the center back, knit 12 sts from the holder, pick up and knit 10 sts along the side of the instep, k12 on instep needle, pick up and knit 10 sts along the other side of the instep, knit 12 sts from the other holder—56 sts.

Next 4 rows With C, knit.

Next row (make welt) With WS facing, *slip the first st from the left-hand to the right-hand needle. Count 3 ridges down on the WS of garter st rows; pick up and knit the top loop of the first st on this ridge, pass the slipped st over the new st; rep from * to the end of the row. (See page 31 for step-by-step photos.)

Next 8 rows Attach A. Knit. Cut A.

Next 2 rows With C, knit. Cut C.

Shape sole

With RS facing, slip first 22 sts onto right hand needle. Attach B and k12 sts, turn. *K11, k2tog (i.e. knit 1 A and 1 C tog), turn; rep from * until all C sts are worked—12 sts rem on needle. K2tog across the row.

Cut yarn leaving a 6" (15.2 cm) tail and, with a yarn needle, pass the tail through the sts on needle and pull tight.

Finishing

Pull "ribbons" to RS of booties as for hat.

Sew the back seam.

Weave in all ends.

With B, make a 3-st I-cord tie (page 30) 18" (45.7 cm) long. Weave the tie through the eyelets and knot each end to keep the cord from slipping through eyelets. Tie in a bow.

A knitted welt (yellow) defines and shapes the top of the bootie.

Dots and Ruffles

Design by Debby Ware

This extraordinary hat-and-bootie set is more challenging to knit but it's worth it. Baby will be the center of attention whenever she wears this sweet concoction!

Seed stitch pattern

Row 1 *K1, p1; rep from * to end of row.

Row 2 Purl each knit stitch and knit each purl stitch.

Rep Row 2.

HAT

This hat is worked in the round. Switch to double pointed needles when the stitches no longer fit comfortably on the circular needle.

Brim

With circular needle and B, cast on 90 sts. Join, being careful not to twist sts. Place a marker on the needle to indicate the beg of rnd, and slip the marker every rnd.

Rnd 1 Purl.

Rnd 2 Attach A. *K1 B, k1 A; rep from * to the end of the rnd.

Rnd 3 With B, *k1, sl 1; rep from * to the end of the rnd.

Rnds 4–12 *K1 B, p1 A; rep from * to the end of the rnd. Cut A.

Rnds 13 and 14 With B, knit one rnd, then purl one rnd.

Ruffle

Next (Inc) rnd *K2, k1f&b; rep from * to the end of the rnd—120 sts.

With B, work seed stitch for 2¼" (5.7 cm). Cut B.

Next rnd Attach A. Knit 1 rnd, then BO all sts pwise.

Crown

Holding the hat with RS facing, bend the ruffle down toward you and expose the join between bottom of the ruffle and the top of the ribbing. With C, pick up and knit 1 st in each "upward" loop at this join—90 sts. With C, work in St st for 2¼" (5.7 cm), or until you have "cleared" the top of the ruffle.

Next (Dec setup) rnd *K8, k2tog, pm; rep from * around—81 sts.

Knit 4 rnds.

Next (Dec) rnd *K to 2 sts before the marker, k2tog; rep from * around—72 sts.

Rep the Dec rnd every fifth rnd twice more, then every fourth rnd twice, every third rnd once and every second rnd once, removing the dec markers on the last rnd—18 sts rem.

K2tog until 6 sts rem.

Cut yarn, leaving a 6" (15.2 cm) tail. Using a yarn needle, thread the tail through the rem sts on the needles. Pull the yarn, gathering sts tightly together, then secure the tail on the WS of hat.

Pom-pom

Make one pom-pom using all 3 colors of hat. Wrap the three yarns around a 3" (7.6 cm) piece of cardboard 50 to 60 times. Cut a 12" (30.5 cm) strand of A. Slip the loops off the cardboard and use the strand of yarn to tie a very tight knot around the loops. Cut through the loops of yarn on either side of the tied knot, and shake the pom-pom hard to fluff it out. Trim the ends evenly.

Finishing

With B, embroider 3-wrap French knots (page 31) all around crown, spaced as desired.

Attach the pom-pom to the peak of the hat.

Weave in all ends.

With C, embroider French knots evenly spaced around, going through both the ruffle and crown fabric, thereby attaching the ruffle to the lower portion of the crown and creating "pockets."

Two-color ribbing makes a snug brim.

BOOTIES

These booties are knitted flat from the cuff down, then seamed. For ease in working, a third needle can be used for the first several rows of the foot shaping; this can be a double-pointed needle if you choose.

Cuff

With smaller needles and A, CO 41 sts. Cut A.

Next 8 rows Attach B, and work in k1, p1 rib. Cut B.

Work k1, p1 ribbing for 8 rows. Cut B.

Next (eyelet) row Attach A. K2, *yo, k2tog, k4; rep from * to last 3 sts, ending last rep yo, k2tog, k1.

Next row (WS) With A, purl 1 row. Cut A.

Next 6 rows Attach C, and work in St st.

Instep

Next row K28, turn. Put the 13 unworked sts on a holder.

Next row P15, turn. Put the 13 unworked sts on another holder.

Next 8 rows Work in St st on these 15 sts only. Cut C.

Evenly spaced French knots secure the ruffle to the sides of the hat forming little pockets.

Foot

Next row With RS facing, attach B at the center back, knit 13 sts from holder, pick up and knit 7 sts along the side of the instep, k15 on instep needle, pick up and knit 7 sts along the other side of instep, knit 13 sts from other holder—55 sts.

Next 10 rows Work in garter stitch for 10 rows.

Welt

Next row (make welt) With WS facing, *slip the first st from the left-hand to the right-hand needle. Count 3 ridges down on the WS of garter st rows; pick up and knit the top loop of the first st on this ridge, pass the slipped st over the new st; rep from * to the end of the row.

Cut B and attach A.

Sole

Next row (RS) K27, pm, k28.

Next 5 rows Knit to marker, slip marker, k2tog, knit to end—50 sts rem.

BO.

Finishing

With B, make 10 small French knots on top of instep of each bootie.

Sew the sole and back seams.

Weave in all ends.

Knit a 3-st I-cord tie approx 22" (55.9 cm) long. Thread the I-cord tie through the eyelets. Make a small knot at each end of the tie to keep it from slipping out.

Double-pointed needles

Double-pointed needles come in sets of four or more. Stitches are cast on continuously from one needle to the next. One needle is used to knit off the stitches that are divided among the other needles. As the last stitch is knitted off a needle, that needle then becomes the working needle.

1. Cast on the stitches onto one needle and then divide them equally or as directed in the project directions among three needles. Arrange the needles in a triangle with the first cast-on stitch on the left and the last cast-on stitch on the right. Make sure the cast-on edges are all facing the center of the triangle and are not twisted.

2. Using the fourth needle, knit the first stitch of the first needle (first cast-on stitch), pulling the yarn firmly to avoid a gap (top).

3. Continue knitting the stitches off the first needle. When the first needle is empty, use it to knit the stitches off the second needle, and so on. When you reach your cast-on tail again, you have completed the first round.

4. Slip a split-coil stitch marker after the last stitch, pulling the yarn through the marker to hold it in place (a solid ring marker will fall off the needle tip). Slip the marker after each round.

I-cord

Narrow knitted tubes, called I-cords, are so useful for tying little booties on Baby's tootsies or for tying a hat in place under a plump chin. They can also be used for embellishments.

1. Cast on the number of stitches needed (usually 2 to 4).

2. Knit the stitches, but do not turn.

3. Slip the stitches from the right-hand needle back to the left hand needle. (If using double-pointed needles, leave the stitches on the same needle and slide them to the other end.)

4. Bring the yarn across the back of the stitches and pull tight. Knit the next row (middle).

5. Repeat steps 3 and 4 until the cord is the desired length.

6. Break the yarn, leaving a 6" (15.2 cm) tail. Use a yarn needle to draw the tail through the remaining stitches.

Knitted welt

Raised ridges, or welts, add a decorative element to a project, and they can also be used to emphasize a design line, such as the dividing line between the sides and crown of a hat or the rim of a bootie sole. With this method, the welt is created as you knit.

1. With wrong side facing, slip the first stitch from the left-hand to the right-hand needle.

2. Count 3 ridges down on the wrong side of the rows; pick up and knit the top loop of the first stitch on this ridge.

3. Pass the slipped stitch over the new stitch.

4. Repeat steps 1 to 3 for every stitch in the welt row.

Grafting

Grafting, also called kitchener stitch, weaves together two rows of "live" stitches (not bound off), resulting in an invisible joining. Using a yarn needle, you stitch the rows together, following the path of the stitches.

1. Cut the working yarn, leaving a tail about 18" (46 cm) long. Leave the